PRAISE Forward

Devotions Of Prayer, Poetry, and Purpose

Synthia Shelby

PRAISE Forward
Devotions of Prayer, Poetry, and Purpose

Copyright ©2021 by Synthia Shelby
Published by Shelby Publishing

Printed in the United States of America

All rights reserved. No part of this book may be reproduced or transmitted in any form or by any means included but not limited to information storage and retrieval systems, electronic, mechanical, photocopy, recording, etc. without written permission of the publisher.

All scripture quotations are taken from the Holy Bible, New International Version®, NIV®. Copyright © 1973, 1978, 1984, 2011 by Biblica, Inc.® Used by permission of Zondervan. All rights reserved worldwide. www.zondervan.com The "NIV" and "New International Version" are trademarks registered in the United States Patent and Trademark Office by Biblica, Inc.®

THANK YOU
for your purchase!

To receive bonus content,
visit www.synthiashelby.com

For God, my family, my tribe, and future generations

Contents

Introduction 1

Section I - Prayer 4

    Prayer Changes Things 6

    Windows of Heaven 9

    Stir It Up! 13

    When Trouble Comes 16

    Step Up 19

    Pain to Purpose 22

    Stand 25

    Trust Me 28

    Healed 31

    Covered 34

Section II - Grateful 38

    Helping Hands 40

    Love Journey 43

    Everyday Blessings 46

    Valued 49

    Positivity 52

    Give and Go 55

    Fail Forward 58

    Be Spectacular 61

Reaching Out 64
Eyes on Jesus 67

Section III - Hush 70
Pause 72
Warning Signs 75
Listen 78
Out of Control 81
Calm Down 84
In the Dark 87
Provision 90
God knows 93
Reflection 96
Never Forget 99

Section IV - Self-Care 102
Enough 104
Temple Maintenance 107
Power 110
Push 113
Help Wanted 116
Courage 119
Investments 122
Spring Cleaning 125
Steady Progress 128
Fill Up 131

Section V - Love 134

    You See Me 136

    What A Friend 139

    God Is in Control! 142

    Unbroken 146

    Time Changes Things 149

    Obedience Detected 152

    Self-Love 155

    Speak 158

    Jesus Will Fix It 161

    Lean on Me 164

Section VI - Joy 168

    Sing 170

    Still Here 173

    Soar 176

    Choices 179

    Hallelujah Anyhow 182

    With Us 185

    No Fear 188

    Inventory 191

    Victory 194

    Shine 197

Introduction

Now faith is confidence in what we hope for and assurance about what we do not see. Hebrews 11:1 (NIV)

When we use our faith and put it into action, this is when the real work begins. Action takes hard work, perseverance, commitment, and faith. I have wavered many times in all of those areas and that is why it has taken me so long to publish this book.

The blessing is that God has been walking with me every step of the way since I first started writing poetry. I was in a very dark place due to a series of poor choices on my part and contemplating suicide. God spoke to me even though I did not want to listen. In my heart and soul, I needed hope. I had a choice between living and dying one night. He whispered and gave me poetry to save my life.

No, I did not write anything profound but simply started writing. I poured my pain onto paper and released it. God renewed my faith and joy, moment by moment. He opened my eyes to see what was right in front of me. God taught me to trust him through life's storms. My life, like yours, is a series of good, bad, awful, and great events. It is only by faith that we will make it to the other side.

Over two years ago, I conceived this book, but I have been writing it my entire life. Inside, you will find my testimonies of hope, anger, sorrow, and joy. I pray that this book will move you out of darkness, inspire you to dream, and empower you to take action towards your goals. I hope this book will be the guide that God will use to open your heart. As you read and reflect, I want you to find the light that shines in you!

I challenge you to take your time with this book as you would an old friend. Take your time to 'Sip with the Savior'. Listen closely to the words and treasure them as you go through life's adventures. Allow them to wrap around your soul as you inhale your purpose and exhale your pain. Do not be in a hurry, but know joy lies in the little rest stops and detours along the way. With faith, you can accomplish anything. So, have faith that God is with you, will guide you, and will never leave you.

Remember, I have not always been where I am today. I am also not finished with my journey and neither are you. Stop thinking that you have to be perfect to follow your path. I am broken in many places, but it is through those cracks that God is working on you. It is through those cracks that he has provided healing, praise, purpose, and testimony. My light and yours shines brighter through our cracks. My cracks help me to know that I must follow my mission of spreading the good news of Jesus.

Although life brings many storms, the way out is to PRAISE! PRAISE implies that you are grateful not for the trial and tragedy, but for the lessons, the trials gave you. PRAISE reminds you that in spite of the storm, it did not blow you away. You are still standing! PRAISE says that you are able to put one foot in front of the other. PRAISE shouts that your faith is not gone and that you are still trusting God. PRAISE means that in spite of ALL you have been through that you will keep going. When you are tempted to give up, use this book to press and PRAISE Forward!

Section I
Prayer

"Lord, thank you for reminding me that my name is Chosen, Conqueror, and Victorious. Thank you for listening to my pain and joy. Forgive me for running away and being too busy to pray. Today, I turn my face to you. Please bless those who are hurting. Heal our world and guide us back to loving one another. Help me to move in the right direction. I need you. Help me to not only read these words and scriptures, but to apply them to my life. I want to listen and obey. In Jesus name, Amen."

2 Chronicles 7:14 – If my people, who are called by my name, will humble themselves and pray and seek my face and turn from their wicked ways, then will I hear from heaven, and I will forgive their sin and will heal their land.

Prayer Changes Things

Open your mouth.
Have a conversation
With the Master.
He's been waiting
To hear from you.

He's a Healer,
Deliverer,
Anchor,
Shepherd,
And Savior.

Need something?
He's got it.

Give him
Your heart.
He'll give you
Unending love.

Give him
Your worries.
He'll give you
His peace.

Give him
Your praise.
He'll send you
Blessings and Favor.

Have a little talk
With Jesus.
He'll listen
No matter
The hour.

2 Chronicles 7:14 – If my people, who are called by my name, will humble themselves and pray and seek my face and turn from their wicked ways, then will I hear from heaven, and I will forgive their sin and will heal their land.

Prayer Changes Things

I bet you keep saying that you are waiting on God, but he is waiting on you. He is waiting for you to talk to him. Take a minute and reflect about your day. Thank him for the lessons you have learned this week, month, or year. Ask him for wisdom.

_____
_____
_____
_____
_____
_____
_____
_____
_____
_____
_____
_____
_____
_____
_____
_____
_____

When I Hear My Mama Pray

I know I'm supposed to be still.
It is a Holy time not to be
interrupted or taken lightly.
She teaches me how to be humble and
to patiently wait on God's perfect will.

When I Hear My Mama Pray

I see her touch
the windows of heaven.
She connects with the Father, Awesome
Redeemer, and Great I Am. His beaming
face surrounds her with Joy and holds
her trembling hand.

When I Hear My Mama Pray

My soul is filled with love because
She knows my Daddy, too.
She's resting in his giant arms.
He will always see her through. Smiling
between each teardrop because He will
wipe each one away. He's holding back
the consuming pain, giving her strength
for one more day.

When I Hear My Mama Pray

She has never forgotten to praise Him
during the seasons of Joy, so she
understands how to stay rooted
in times filled with pain.
I know that everything is going
to be alright when God calls her
home and her day becomes night.
It will be the only time
that I won't hear my mama pray.

- Dedicated to those who have a loved one diagnosed with a critical illness. -

2 Chronicles 7:14 – *If my people, who are called by my name, will humble themselves and pray and seek my face and turn from their wicked ways, then will I hear from heaven, and I will forgive their sin and will heal their land.*

Windows of Heaven

What sickness or pain do you need to give to God? Tell God in the lines below what you need. Write a prayer and release all the pain you have been holding inside.

_____

_____

_____

_____

_____

_____

_____

_____

_____

_____

_____

_____

_____

_____

_____

_____

_____

Stir It Up!

Don't allow evil to be good. Don't allow wrong to be right. Don't allow the conversations or divisiveness make you forget that we all need to be unified for a common cause or we will all fall. Don't put your head in the sand. Silence is not an option! Stir It Up! Don't believe that if you don't fight for the rights of others, that yours are covered. The target is on you next. Get involved. Never allow fear to keep you hostage. Never believe that one group has the right to oppress another. It is never acceptable to be prejudiced, racist, biased or just plain hateful. Use your voice, your position, and your privilege to make some noise!

2 Chronicles 7:14 – If my people, who are called by my name, will humble themselves and pray and seek my face and turn from their wicked ways, then will I hear from heaven, and I will forgive their sin and will heal their land.

Stir It Up!

If you are ready to stop injustice in your neighborhood, community, or the world, then be prepared to act. How will you use your voice to make a difference? Who will you contact? Where will you go? What do you need to do to make sure that this does not continue on your watch? Why is this important to you?

_____
_____
_____
_____
_____
_____
_____
_____
_____
_____
_____
_____
_____
_____

Praise Forward

When Trouble Comes...

Will you run away
Or grow closer
day-by-day?

Will you allow fear
To take control
Or let your prayers
Grow strong and bold?

Will you let the storms
pull you under the waves
Or stretch your faith
By standing courageous
And brave?

It will either
Crush you
Or
Elevate you.

Which will
You choose?

2 Chronicles 7:14 – If my people, who are called by my name, will humble themselves and pray and seek my face and turn from their wicked ways, then will I hear from heaven, and I will forgive their sin and will heal their land.

When Trouble Comes...

Prayer is your weapon! Reflect on your struggles. Look up scriptures that are about strength, courage, and wisdom. Write out your prayers and add your scriptures. Ask God to help you fight in the spirit.

Step Up

It is time to put fear out of your house, heart and mind. When he knocks on your door, don't let him in! Plan, Act and Do something that will destroy him. Take a risk and stand up for what you believe in, go back to school, speak up at a meeting, join a ministry, open your heart to love again, mentor a child, forgive someone or yourself, or simply laugh and learn from your mistakes. Fear wants to paralyze you, but your mistakes, trials and tragedies will merely grow you and give you a testimony to share.

2 Chronicles 7:14 – If my people, who are called by my name, will humble themselves and pray and seek my face and turn from their wicked ways, then will I hear from heaven, and I will forgive their sin and will heal their land.

Step Up

What are you ready to do? Who are you ready to become? What are you ready to give up? Take a step of faith and say it aloud. You have been complaining too long. Now, is the time for you to push! Stop hiding behind others and walk in your truth.

_____

_____

_____

_____

_____

_____

_____

_____

_____

_____

_____

_____

_____

_____

_____

_____

Pain to Purpose

Whatever you
Are going through
Whenever you don't
Know what to do

Take time
Sit still
Talk to The Master
He'll take the wheel

Tell Him
about your
Loneliness
Baggage
And Mess

He wants
To know about
Your Pain
Grief
And Distress

Stop trying
To do it all
On Your own

Let God
Be God

Remember He's
On the throne

If you let Him
He'll take you from
Pride to Peace
Tears to Testimonies
Fear to Favor
Chaos to Courage

If you let Him
He'll take you from
Loss to Love
Sorrow to Strength
Weakness to Worship
Damaged to Disciplined

Whatever you
Are going through
Whenever you don't
Know what to do

Take time
Sit still
Talk to
The Master
Let Him Take the wheel

2 Chronicles 7:14 – If my people, who are called by my name, will humble themselves and pray and seek my face and turn from their wicked ways, then will I hear from heaven, and I will forgive their sin and will heal their land.

Pain to Purpose

Capture what you have gone through and write it down. Get the pain out and on the paper. Release it! What will you do with it? Will you write a blog, a poem, or a book? Do you want to share it with the world or is it just for you? It's your pain, your purpose, and your power.

_____
_____
_____
_____
_____
_____
_____
_____
_____
_____
_____
_____
_____
_____
_____
_____

Stand

Do you worry about how you will accomplish your goals? How will you be enough? Why has God chosen you? Feeling a bit discouraged? Pray, Go to the Word, Listen, and Believe. Our God is always there. Whatever he purposed you to do, he has provided the tools for your success. Stop listening to the enemy whisper doubt and discouragement. Allow God's Word to remind you that you serve a Mighty God. He is Alpha and Omega. He is the Bright and Morning Star. He will give you strength, courage, boldness, and anything else you need to accomplish what he has set before you.

2 Chronicles 7:14 – If my people, who are called by my name, will humble themselves and pray and seek my face and turn from their wicked ways, then will I hear from heaven, and I will forgive their sin and will heal their land.

Stand

What were the circumstances when you felt most alone, and God provided comfort? Who or what did God send to help you? I dare you to stand and remember that God is always with you.

_____

_____

_____

_____

_____

_____

_____

_____

_____

_____

_____

_____

_____

_____

_____

Praise Forward

Trust Me

I woke you up and
Gave you a brand
New day.

I will protect
And guide you
Along the way.

Don't give up
No matter how
Hard life seems.

Never forget
That you're on
The Savior's team.

You may suffer
Some injuries or
Even foul out.

When It looks
The worst, trust
Don't doubt.

I'm always
There holding
Your hand.

Even when YOU
can't see, I'll
Help you stand.

I promise
To love, guide,
And keep you.

I am the light
Which will take
You through.

2 Chronicles 7:14 – If my people, who are called by my name, will humble themselves and pray and seek my face and turn from their wicked ways, then will I hear from heaven, and I will forgive their sin and will heal their land.

Trust Me

What do you trust in without question? Why do you find it so hard to trust God? If you want to trust, then you have to invest in your relationship. God needs you to spend time, listen, and get to know him.

Healed

Though storm clouds form
Though trouble rages all around
He who suffered a crown of thorns
Covers us when life knocks us down

No more sickness
No more pain
Jesus loves us no matter our mess
He holds us during heartache's rain

When we are weak
When we are forlorn
He is the courage that we seek
Lifts us away from Satan's scorn

No more sickness
No more pain
Jesus loves us no matter our mess
He holds us during heartache's rain

2 Chronicles 7:14 – If my people, who are called by my name, will humble themselves and pray and seek my face and turn from their wicked ways, then will I hear from heaven, and I will forgive their sin and will heal their land.

Healed

What junk are you carrying around about your past? Why do you feel this way? God can take away your mess and help you walk with your head held high. If you really want to let go and change your life, then how will you stop walking backwards and move forward with Jesus?

_____
_____
_____
_____
_____
_____
_____
_____
_____
_____
_____
_____
_____
_____
_____

Covered

Dear Lord,

Thank you for the promise that you will be with us. Thank you for your protection during racial injustice, death, danger, discouragement, and distractions. Thank you for not allowing the storm to wipe us out.

Sometimes we forget that we are not alone. We forget and try to do life on our own. Forgive us for our amnesia. Forgive us for our many complaints. Forgive us for not following you.

Oh, great God, have mercy on us. Help us use words that affirm not anger. Help us speak purpose not pain. Lead us to truth not tall tales. Allow faith to overtake not fear. Steer us to be warriors not weaklings.

We praise you for answering this prayer. We praise you for your love, grace, mercy, and power! We praise you for the mountain of testimonies that will come from our tests. We praise you for being our shepherd, comforter, and anchor.

In Jesus name, Amen.

2 Chronicles 7:14 – If my people, who are called by my name, will humble themselves and pray and seek my face and turn from their wicked ways, then will I hear from heaven, and I will forgive their sin and will heal their land.

Covered

Write a thank you note to God for what he has protected you from today, this week, or this year. Fill it with as many details as you can. Share the note with a family member or friend that may need encouragement when they are experiencing a difficult season.

_____
_____
_____
_____
_____
_____
_____
_____
_____
_____
_____
_____
_____
_____
_____
_____
_____
_____
_____

SECTION II
GRATEFUL

"Daddy, I am grateful for your kindness. I am grateful for another chance to try again, even though I don't deserve it. I am grateful for your strength in fighting for racial justice and dismantling systemic racism. I am grateful for you teaching us that we are greater than our differences. I am grateful that you love the lost and the least. You set the model for the rest of us. I am grateful for those who stand for justice and make our world one without hate. All it takes is a little bit of faith. I am grateful to know your word and be part of spreading your message of light and love. You give me hope and courage. I praise your Holy name!"

Psalm 9:1 – I will give thanks to you Lord, with all my heart; I will tell of all your wonderful deeds.

Helping Hands

We didn't make it this far on our own. We stand on the shoulders of family, friends, prayer warriors, ancestors, activists, and even ditch diggers who tried to stop us. We didn't pull ourselves up. We had someone motivate us through kind words or an open door. Remember that the next time someone needs your help.

Psalm 9:1 – I will give thanks to you Lord, with all my heart; I will tell of all your wonderful deeds.

Helping Hands

Allow your heart to be open today to the needs of others. Write the name of a person you know has a need and ask God to show you how to help.

_____
_____
_____
_____
_____
_____
_____
_____
_____
_____
_____
_____
_____
_____
_____
_____

Love Journey

Let people know you by your love! You say you know Jesus, but how do you love? You say you are kind and caring, but how do you love? Open your heart and mind to see the good in others. Learn to love! Push through the baggage of your past and the drama of your present and walk towards the love of God, family, and friends who want to hold you close. Take a chance on giving and receiving love.

Psalm 9:1 – I will give thanks to you Lord, with all my heart; I will tell of all your wonderful deeds.

Love Journey

How will you love today? Who needs to know you love them not by what you say, but by what you do? Keep your heart open and receive the love that comes your way.

_____
_____
_____
_____
_____
_____
_____
_____
_____
_____
_____
_____
_____
_____
_____

Everyday Blessings

Don't Delay!

Say, "I Love You!" while you can.
Give the gift of you,
your time, your presence.
Help someone you don't know.
Practice gratefulness.

Don't be Shaken!

Pray for others.
Make every heartbeat count.
Life can change in a blink.
When it looks different
Than what you were expecting,
Know God will take you through.

Psalm 9:1 – I will give thanks to you Lord, with all my heart; I will tell of all your wonderful deeds.

Everyday Blessings

Why are you waiting? Mail the card. Make the phone call. Forgive the person who hurt you the most. Take time to let the pain go and love who is right in front of you. Write down your burdens and give them to God, today.

_____
_____
_____
_____
_____
_____
_____
_____
_____
_____
_____
_____
_____
_____
_____
_____

Valued

No matter your race, gender, height, weight, economic status, relationship status, or political affiliation, YOU Are Valued! No matter what you have done in your past, YOU Are Valued! No matter the amount of guilt, depression, fear, or doubt you hold onto daily, YOU Are Valued!

God's love covers all of us! Trust Him enough to let him in. He will change your life by changing your perspective. No matter what others say, God cares and YOU Are Valued!

Psalm 9:1 – I will give thanks to you Lord, with all my heart; I will tell of all your wonderful deeds.

Valued

Create your own words of affirmation. Write it down and then post it at home, work, or school in a prominent place. Repeat it every day reminding yourself that YOU Are Valued. (Examples: Victorious, Loved, and Courageous)

_____

_____

_____

_____

_____

_____

_____

_____

_____

_____

_____

_____

_____

_____

Positivity

Life is not perfect and neither are you. It is okay. Life is real, messy, and full of possibilities. You have the ability to laugh, move, and dance through each day! Be grateful when you have someone that cares about you. You can smell the beauty of a new day. You can hear the giggles of children, the chirping of birds, feel the touch of a morning breeze, or hope beyond what you can see.

Psalm 9:1 – I will give thanks to you Lord, with all my heart; I will tell of all your wonderful deeds.

Positivity

Take a moment this week and celebrate who and what is a positive part of your life. Write them down for seven days and see how amazing you feel. It is okay to repeat them. Create a list, a picture, a story, a song, a poem, or a prayer.

_____
_____
_____
_____
_____
_____
_____
_____
_____
_____
_____
_____
_____
_____
_____
_____

Give and Go

Give
To others
When they are
Hurting or in pain
God works
Through us to
Give
His love
And mend the broken

Go!
Spread kindness
And love
Go!
Serve God
By serving others
Go!
Lift up someone
When they are down

Psalm 9:1 – I will give thanks to you Lord, with all my heart; I will tell of all your wonderful deeds.

Give and Go

Get off your sofa and off your butt. Take the time to make a difference in your family, community, and world. What can you give this week to make someone's life better? Where can you go to make a difference?

_____
_____
_____
_____
_____
_____
_____
_____
_____
_____
_____
_____
_____
_____

Fail Forward

Did you make a mistake yesterday or a colossal one last week? Do not allow it to destroy your confidence. Use it as manure to grow. Reflect on how you can do better and make changes. Allow it to motivate you to be more focused and productive.

Psalm 9:1 – I will give thanks to you Lord, with all my heart; I will tell of all your wonderful deeds.

Fail Forward

What lessons can you learn from a recent mistake? Write a prayer of thanks for the lessons you learned. Identify some things you can do to keep someone else from making the same mistake.

Be Spectacular

Share a hug, smile, kind word, card, email, visit, or a phone call. Hold open a door, give someone a lift to a destination, pay for someone's meal, or hold someone's hand. Be available when someone needs you to listen or help a child yearning for love. Open your mind and heart today so you can influence the world through your actions, instead of your mouth.

Psalm 9:1 – I will give thanks to you Lord, with all my heart; I will tell of all your wonderful deeds.

Be Spectacular

Allow your heart to be open today to the needs of others. Write out the name of a person you know has a need and ask God to show you how to help. Identify steps you can take to be spectacular daily, weekly, monthly, or yearly.

_____

_____

_____

_____

_____

_____

_____

_____

_____

_____

_____

_____

_____

_____

_____

_____

Reaching Out

It doesn't
Take much
To change
A life.

It's the little things
That mean so much.
Be grateful
That you have another
Day to reach out.

I dare you!
Share a smile.
Provide a meal.
Send a card.
Spend time with
A neighbor.

Psalm 9:1 – I will give thanks to you Lord, with all my heart; I will tell of all your wonderful deeds.

Reaching Out

Think about the resources you have that could help someone. How could you be the answer to their prayer?

_____
_____
_____
_____
_____
_____
_____
_____
_____
_____
_____
_____
_____
_____
_____
_____
_____

Eyes on Jesus

You can walk on water. I believe it because I've done it and so can you. I've walked on water when my father abandoned us, when my mother and grandmother died 10 months apart, when my heart was shattered, when… I was able to walk on the water of faith, hope, courage, peace, and love. When you keep your eyes on Jesus the storms will come, but they can't take you down. Where are your eyes?

Psalm 9:1 – I will give thanks to you Lord, with all my heart; I will tell of all your wonderful deeds.

Eyes on Jesus

Do you want to walk on water? What keeps you distracted from living above the circumstances? What do you need to release or walk through to help you refocus?

_____

_____

_____

_____

_____

_____

_____

_____

_____

_____

_____

_____

_____

_____

Praise Forward

Section III
Hush

"Lord, right now, I'm feeling lost and all alone. Everywhere I turn, the world feels like it's falling apart and something else seems to go wrong. Please guide me, lead me, and order my steps. Take fear away and replace it with your peace. Take away the darkness that feels like it's chasing me wherever I go. I am placing my trust in you, not my circumstances. I will remember your promise to be with me wherever I go. I will not doubt you. You told me to be strong and courageous. You said that you will fight my battles. You have not given me the spirit of fear. I will hold my head up and walk boldly because of your protection, provision, and love. Thank you for being my God. Thank you for being my anchor in the midst of the storm."

Philippians 4:6 – Do not be anxious about anything, but in every situation, by prayer and petition, with thanksgiving, present your requests to God.

Pause

Quiet
Stillness
Reflection

Hoping
Trusting
Dreaming

Letting Go
Resting
Breathing

Philippians 4:6 – Do not be anxious about anything, but in every situation, by prayer and petition, with thanksgiving, present your requests to God.

Pause

When was the last time you took a pause in your day, week, month, or year? Evaluate if you need to put a pause on anything in your life that is not serving a purpose.

_____
_____
_____
_____
_____
_____
_____
_____
_____
_____
_____
_____
_____
_____
_____
_____
_____

Warning Signs

Danger
Danger
Danger
You're heading for a fall.

Stop
Yield
Listen
You don't pay attention at all.

Gotta help
Gotta do
Gotta move
They can't do it without me.

Running here
Running there
Running everywhere
Where's the victory?

Never get so busy
That you forget
To hit the pause button
Be still, listen, and rest.

In the quiet moments
You hear life clearly.
A baby's laugh.
A bird's chirp.

God's whisper
And love beckons.

In the quiet moments
Your vision clears
To see joy in
The face of a friend
Kindness in the touch
Of a loved one
Or patience with yourself.

Slow down.
Be still, listen, and rest

Philippians 4:6 – Do not be anxious about anything, but in every situation, by prayer and petition, with thanksgiving, present your requests to God.

Warning Signs

When you think you need to fix everything for everybody, take a moment and pray. What is God whispering in your spirit or directing you to do through the scriptures?

_____
_____
_____
_____
_____
_____
_____
_____
_____
_____
_____
_____
_____
_____
_____

Listen

Hush
Be quiet
Be still
God is talking...

Birds chirping
Animals rustling
Breeze blowing
God whispers...

Sun shining
Thunder rolling
Rain dancing
God moves...

Troubles
Trials
Testimonies
God prepares...

Crying
Questioning
Wondering
God hears...

Laughter
Love
Lessons
God guides...

Open heart
Yielded will
Mind focused
God answers...

Hush
Be quiet
Be still
God is talking...

Philippians 4:6 – Do not be anxious about anything, but in every situation, by prayer and petition, with thanksgiving, present your requests to God.

Listen

What places in your home or community help you hear life better? Analyze the distractions you have in your life that keep you from listening to what you need to hear.

_____
_____
_____
_____
_____
_____
_____
_____
_____
_____
_____
_____
_____
_____
_____
_____
_____
_____
_____

Out of Control

Back and forth
Forth and back.
Storms are all
Around you.
You can't seem
To get on track.

Frustrated
Irritated
Complicated
Agitated
Describes your
Present state.

You're on a
Hamster wheel,
Can't seem
To get off.
Can't figure
Life out,
Utterly lost.

But God
Is still
On the throne!
He'll never
Ever leave
You alone.

Stop trying
To do everything
On your own!
Stop being
So busy and
Find time
To be Still.

It's only
In the
Quiet moments
That you'll
Hear the
Master's will.

Open your
Bible and
Allow God
To speak.
Pray, study
And he'll
Provide peace.

Stop trying
To do everything
On your own!
Stop being
So busy and
Find time
To be still.

Philippians 4:6 – Do not be anxious about anything, but in every situation, by prayer and petition, with thanksgiving, present your requests to God.

Out of Control

Why are you so afraid? When did things get so overwhelming in your life? How can you run toward God with courage?

_____
_____
_____
_____
_____
_____
_____
_____
_____
_____
_____
_____
_____
_____

Calm Down

Hush, child
Stop your squirming
And crying.

I see you
I hear you
I know it hurts.

Hush, child
Remember who I Am
And listen.

I haven't left
I didn't disappear
I know what you need.

Hush, child
Go somewhere, sit down
And lose the attitude.

I feel your pain
I understand your sorrow
I know your story.

I love you
I adore you
I know you are mine.

Hush, child
Come back to me
And I will give your rest.

Philippians 4:6 – Do not be anxious about anything, but in every situation, by prayer and petition, with thanksgiving, present your requests to God.

Calm Down

What will it take for you to be still before God? How will learning to be still help structure your life?

_____
_____
_____
_____
_____
_____
_____
_____
_____
_____
_____
_____
_____
_____
_____
_____
_____
_____

In the Dark

He won't
Fail
He won't
Run away
He is able
To deliver you
When you face giants

He will
Speak
He will
Provide
He is able
To keep you
In deep water

He hears
Your cries
He knows
Your pain
He is able
To guide you
Through the storm

He will
Lift you up
He will
Comfort you
He is able
To heal you
From the pain

Philippians 4:6 – Do not be anxious about anything, but in every situation, by prayer and petition, with thanksgiving, present your requests to God.

In the Dark

What things do you need to let go of in the dark, so you can return to the light? Create a song list that will help you in the dark. Play it and remember that God is with you.

_____
_____
_____
_____
_____
_____
_____
_____
_____
_____
_____
_____
_____
_____
_____
_____
_____
_____
_____

Praise Forward

Provision

In spite of this chaos,
Food still on your table.
Family is safe and healthy.
Friends call to check in.
You realize you're blessed.

In the middle of the madness,
You remember to be grateful:
For your home, kindness,
Patience, peace, and love.
Your time to rest and renew is now.

In the struggle for normal,
You listen, sit still, and pray.

Earn certificates and degrees.
Realize that you are brave,
Brilliant, and bodacious.
Ready to focus on dreams
You forgot yesterday.

In the valley of frustration,
You stop. Inhale…exhale…
And breathe.
Thankful for those working
To keep you safe
So you can try again.
You stop. Inhale…exhale…
And breathe.

Philippians 4:6 – Do not be anxious about anything, but in every situation, by prayer and petition, with thanksgiving, present your requests to God.

Provision

Using a shoebox, decorate it, and label it: Provision. Every time God blesses you with a specific provision write a note and put it in the box. After 30 days, go back and review the wonderful things God has provided in your life.

God knows

My junk
My mess
My insecurities
My fear
And whispers, I love you.

My failures
My pain
My tears
My wants
And whispers, I'll sustain you.

My treachery
My unbelief
My foul language
My bad attitude
And whispers, I forgive you.

My name
My journey
My hopes
My destiny
And whispers, You are My child.

I am grateful that
I serve a Mighty God
Bigger than my problems,
Stronger than I am weak,
Loves me in spite of myself,
Forgives me, and guides me
Through life's deep, murky waters.

He knows who I really am
Sees behind my masks
And whispers…
And whispers…

Philippians 4:6 – Do not be anxious about anything, but in every situation, by prayer and petition, with thanksgiving, present your requests to God.

God Knows

What masks are you hiding behind, today? Write a letter to the person you want to be and tell them what you are going to do right now so you can meet them.

_____
_____
_____
_____
_____
_____
_____
_____
_____
_____
_____
_____
_____
_____
_____
_____
_____
_____

Praise Forward

Reflection

Life is precious
Don't take it for granted
Make the most of each hour
Let nothing and no one steal your joy

Time owes you nothing
Grab what's in front of you
Soak it in and hold it carefully
Before it blows away

No dress rehearsals
Life doesn't have slow motion
More like terminal velocity
Treasure it, wisely

Enjoy quiet moments
Listen to butterflies sing
Watch moonbeams dance
and inhale the kiss of each day

Pray about everything
Push past adversity
Praise your way through
Pause to relish love

Philippians 4:6 – Do not be anxious about anything, but in every situation, by prayer and petition, with thanksgiving, present your requests to God.

Reflection

What have you been too busy to enjoy? Who needs your time and attention? Evaluate what is most important and then prioritize your actions.

_____
_____
_____
_____
_____
_____
_____
_____
_____
_____
_____
_____
_____
_____
_____
_____

Never Forget

I'm a Daughter
And Treasure
Of a King.
I'm Chosen
By God.
He knows
My name.

I'm His
Child and He
Will provide.
I'm Redeemed
And Delivered
By the blood.

I'm an Audacious
Warrior for Jesus.
I'm strutting
Through life
With my head
Held high and
My armor on.

Never forget
Who you are!

Philippians 4:6 – Do not be anxious about anything, but in every situation, by prayer and petition, with thanksgiving, present your requests to God.

Never Forget

In this section, reread the poem God Knows. Thinking about God Knows and Never Forget, identify who are you in Christ?

_____
_____
_____
_____
_____
_____
_____
_____
_____
_____
_____
_____
_____
_____
_____
_____

Section IV
Self-Care

"Lord, I am drained, overwhelmed, and exhausted. Every time I think I can rest something else happens. When will it stop? How do I deal with it? I cannot do this on my own. I need you...I need you, Lord. You are mighty and merciful. Help me! I come to you Jehovah Jireh: My Provider. Please take all of my fear, anger, hurt, frustration, and trying to be everything for everyone. Take control, Lord. Teach me how to rest in you. I come to you Jehovah Shalom: God of Peace. I know that the battle is not mine, but yours. I give all my worries and my pain over to you."

Matthew 11:28 – "Come to me, all you who are weary and burdened, and I will give you rest."

Enough

If you believe in God, then do not be defeated by what you tell yourself. No longer allow others to have control by what they say to or about you. You are strong, confident, and victorious. Get off the wall of mediocrity. Get out of your emotions. Move into each day with purpose, passion, and positivity. Speak life to yourself and your situation. Believe that God is with you. Know that you are covered and chosen. Walk with your head up. Stand as if you know your daddy is the King of Kings!

Matthew 11:28 – "Come to me, all you who are weary and burdened, and I will give you rest."

Enough

Check in with yourself and write down one to three words to describe how you feel about you. Own those feelings and release any that are negative. For every negative word you wrote down, write three positive ones. Repeat one of those positive words every day to yourself for 21 days.

Temple Maintenance

Smile every day. Pray at every opportunity. Healthy eating is essential. Intellectual conversation is required. 'No' is an integral part of your vocabulary. Sit, breathe, relax and unwind after you have done your best. Forgive those who hurt you. Don't run with the baggage of your past. Forgive yourself and appreciate now. Make room for dreams and imagination. Shine your light for others to see. Trust God for victory.

Matthew 11:28 – "Come to me, all you who are weary and burdened, and I will give you rest."

Temple Maintenance

What is stopping you from taking care of your temple? Write it down and then create a plan that will help you look and be your best self. Identify at least one goal from your plan and focus on it for the next two weeks. Find an accountability partner to report your progress.

_____
_____
_____
_____
_____
_____
_____
_____
_____
_____
_____
_____
_____
_____
_____

Power

Don't let anything or anyone steal your joy. Stop tripping and start strutting like the daughters and sons of a King. Start crowing about your power and purpose, instead of your problems and your pain. Release your bitterness and hold onto the beauty of God's forgiveness. Accept that you are amazing, unique, and a gift to humanity.

Matthew 11:28 – "Come to me, all you who are weary and burdened, and I will give you rest."

Power

Take a moment and think about your power. Where does it come from? Why is it important to recognize that you have it? Write down some ways you can walk in your power and develop it day by day.

_____
_____
_____
_____
_____
_____
_____
_____
_____
_____
_____
_____
_____
_____
_____
_____
_____

Push

GOD
And the world
Do not OWE you
Anything.

STOP
Allowing
Jealousy,
Anger,
Depression,
Or Pity parties To
sideline you.

Get up,
Get busy,
And go after
What you want!

Never
Let anyone
Or anything
Destroy
What God
Has placed
In your heart.

Matthew 11:28 – "Come to me, all you who are weary and burdened, and I will give you rest."

Push

What do you want? Where do you want to be next month or next year? Write out where you want to be and create a strategic plan of how to get there. Remember: You are the only one standing in the way.

_____
_____
_____
_____
_____
_____
_____
_____
_____
_____
_____
_____
_____
_____
_____
_____
_____

Praise Forward

Help Wanted

You can ask for help, I promise. Sometimes life and the things that come at you each day seem too daunting to handle. You are right! They are too much to handle all on your own. This is why God wants you to call on him. His shoulders are never too weak to hold your burdens. His ears are always available for your cries of pain or your shouts of joy. Asking for help is one of the wisest things you can do. Today, post your **Help Wanted** sign with God and allow him to send the resources you need.

Matthew 11:28 – "Come to me, all you who are weary and burdened, and I will give you rest."

Help Wanted

Are you exhausted from trying to take care of everything on your own? Why do you do this? What makes you not ask for help? Write out your thoughts and concerns. Identify small steps you can take to trust God and others to carry some of the load.

_____

_____

_____

_____

_____

_____

_____

_____

_____

_____

_____

_____

_____

_____

_____

_____

Courage

If you only knew…
People think
That I have it
ALL together.
If you only knew…
I am weak but,
I serve a mighty God.

He has me looking
And sounding good.
I cannot do life
On my own.

He told me
To walk by faith,
Pray, trust, and obey
Even when I am afraid.

No matter
How hard
Something looks,
Do it anyway
Because
God is able
To keep you!

Matthew 11:28 – *"Come to me, all you who are weary and burdened, and I will give you rest."*

Courage

What are you afraid of but want to accomplish? When will you take a step towards walking with courage? List some places you want to go or things you want to do that will take a leap of faith. Pick one, pray, and start moving towards your dream. Take it one step at a time.

_____

_____

_____

_____

_____

_____

_____

_____

_____

_____

_____

_____

_____

_____

_____

Investments

You cannot invest in anything if you have not made a deposit. We say we want love, but walk around being angry, nasty, and bitter towards people every day. Your balance is below your capacity to withdraw. We say we need someone to listen and trust us. Yet, we spend our time spreading rumors, lies, or gossiping about people when we know it is wrong. Your Trust/Listening portfolio is in the RED! If you want a return on your investments of love, trust, listening, peace, or joy, you need to make regular deposits in your account.

Matthew 11:28 – "Come to me, all you who are weary and burdened, and I will give you rest."

Investments

Stop fooling yourself by thinking you can say and do anything without paying for it. What do you want out of your life? Look through the mirror of your life and write down your investments. What are you gaining because of them? If you do not like what you see, change it.

_____

_____

_____

_____

_____

_____

_____

_____

_____

_____

_____

_____

_____

_____

_____

_____

_____

Spring Cleaning

Have you tossed out the cobwebs of bad language, laziness, and procrastination? Wipe off the table of regret and replace it with a focus on your future. Vacuum up the pieces of your insecurities and call on the Holy Spirit. Allow God to give you the wisdom, courage, and peace that you seek. Time to get your house in order.

Matthew 11:28 – "Come to me, all you who are weary and burdened, and I will give you rest."

Spring Cleaning

When you let go of junk in your home or spirit, it makes room for better things to take their place. What kind of cleaning do you need to do in your life? Take an inventory and see what you need to let go or keep. Decide if you are really ready to be free.

_____
_____
_____
_____
_____
_____
_____
_____
_____
_____
_____
_____
_____
_____
_____
_____

Praise Forward

Steady Progress

Quit going off course!
Once you know
The right direction,
Plan
Move
And Recognize people
Or Problems that try
To derail you.
Notice the snakes
In the grass that try
To bite you.
Serve
Dream
Love
On purpose!

Matthew 11:28 – "Come to me, all you who are weary and burdened, and I will give you rest."

Steady Progress

Where do you want to go physically, mentally, or spiritually? When will you get there? Why is this important? Put your ideas down and untangle them from your mind. Revisit this page until you see a clear path for your journey.

_____

_____

_____

_____

_____

_____

_____

_____

_____

_____

_____

_____

_____

_____

_____

_____

Fill Up

Encourage Each Other, daily. Fill someone's emptiness with kind words. Offer hope with a smile. Build peace by choosing not to argue. Love beyond race, religion, sexual orientation, and economics. Allow your positivity to change the atmosphere.

Matthew 11:28 – "Come to me, all you who are weary and burdened, and I will give you rest."

Fill Up

Life is hard, sometimes. How can others help you fill your cup? Why can filling up someone else's cup also help you fill your own? A full cup helps you spread more joy with others.

_____
_____
_____
_____
_____
_____
_____
_____
_____
_____
_____
_____
_____
_____
_____
_____
_____
_____

Praise Forward

SECTION V
LOVE

"Oh God! Your love is never-ending. Show others that no matter what they have done, you still love them. Remind them that your gift is free of charge and you are not looking for anything in return. Draw them to your Holy Spirit and wrap them in your presence. Thank you for being the light in our darkness. Thank you for holding us up when our lives are shattered. Thank you for sending joy when we least expect it. Thank you for the love that was given to all of us on Calvary."

1 Corinthians 13:13 – And now these three remain: faith, hope, and love. But the greatest of these is love.

You See Me

Fear
Faults
Failures
Flakiness
Fornication
And yet,
You still love me.

Busyness
Grumbling
Gossiping
Obstinance
Running away
And yet,
You still love me.

Drama
Denial
Doubt
Depression
Disorganization
And yet,
You still love me.

Hateful
Hiding
Horrible
Hurting
And yet,
You still love me.

In spite of all my junk
And all the layers of pain
You peel back my mask.
The real me
lies underneath.
You see all of me.
And yet,
You still love me.

1 Corinthians 13:13 – And now these three remain: faith, hope, and love. But the greatest of these is love.

You See Me

What are you hiding behind your mask? Why do you think you keep it hidden instead of facing it? Ask God to help you deal with it so your tomorrow can be different.

_____
_____
_____
_____
_____
_____
_____
_____
_____
_____
_____
_____
_____
_____
_____
_____
_____

What A Friend

Don't lose hope
Don't walk away
Don't run
Come close
I'm here
Talk to me

Storms
Tragedies
Loss
Pain
Are part
Of the journey

Tough seasons
Yield harvests
Tough seasons
Uncover
Your pain

When you think
All is lost
Courage
Tenacity
Perseverance
Appear

Don't lose hope
Don't walk away
Don't run

Come close
I'm here

Pain
Frustration
Anger
Resentment
You wish
To disappear

Joy
Hope
Peace
Love
Are welcome

Not all
Seasons
Are fun
But each
Is necessary
To grow

Don't lose hope
Don't walk away
Don't run
Come close
I'm here
Talk to me

1 Corinthians 13:13 – And now these three remain: faith, hope, and love. But the greatest of these is love.

What A Friend

How can you draw closer to God? What things do you need to release? Why is this important?

_____
_____
_____
_____
_____
_____
_____
_____
_____
_____
_____
_____
_____
_____
_____
_____
_____
_____
_____

God Is in Control!

Devil, I'm putting you on notice!
You are on notice that I'm going
To stop letting you lead me astray.
I know that the road my Jesus provides
Is the clear and perfect way.
God Is in Control!

Devil, I'm putting you on notice!
You can't control me with worries
About money because I know that
My father is rich in houses and land.
No longer will fear grip my soul
Because my Lord says
He is the strength of my life.
I know that he will be with me
Whether I'm young
Or the days I'm growing old.
God Is in Control!

Devil, I'm putting you on notice!
You can't keep making me think
That I don't deserve happiness or love.
I know that real Love and Joy
Comes from the Master above.
God Is in Control!

If you are struggling with the madness
Of our world today and need a new light
To brighten your pathway,
Then become a warrior for Jesus,
Take your hands off the steering wheel
Vacate your seat, and know that
God Is in Control!

1 Corinthians 13:13 – And now these three remain: faith, hope, and love. But the greatest of these is love.

God Is in Control!

Do you feel like you have to control everything? What keeps you from letting God be in control? Make a list of things you need to give to God..

_____

_____

_____

_____

_____

_____

_____

_____

_____

_____

_____

_____

_____

_____

_____

_____

Unbroken

No matter what we do
Or what we say
God's love always
Makes a way.

He's there during
The good times
As well as
Every storm.

He's there when
We choose
To do right and
Even when we
Choose to do wrong.

Even when our
Mind is scattered

God remains faithful.

Even when we give
Our heart to another
He remains devoted.

No one and nothing can
Separate us from his love
It's unfathomable.

We didn't do anything
To destroy his love.
It's unconditional.

No matter what we do
Or what we say,
God's love always
Makes a way.

1 Corinthians 13:13 – And now these three remain: faith, hope, and love. But the greatest of these is love.

Unbroken

How does God demonstrate his love for you? How do you demonstrate your love for God? Review these scriptures: Isaiah 54:10, Psalm 136:26, and Zephaniah 3:17

What themes did you uncover?

_____
_____
_____
_____
_____
_____
_____
_____
_____
_____
_____
_____
_____
_____
_____

Time Changes Things

I miss her. The woman who always cooked fried chicken, hot water cornbread, and golden fried potatoes fresh from her garden out back.

I miss her making milk gravy in that big ol' cast iron skillet which made your mouth water as you sat eating it all with homemade biscuits.

I miss her. The queen who used to wear her regal crown for all to see and adore. She was always dressed to perfection adorned by her jewels passed down from generations before. The crowns, her hats, her brim blocking the view of anyone who sat behind her on Sunday in their favorite pew.

I miss her singing in my ears, "School days, school days, dear old golden rule days. Readin' Writin' and 'Rithmetic." as she nudged rusty knees, nappy hair, and crusty eyes from the quilt laden bed. "Come on, up and at 'em!"

I miss her sweet country twang and love that I heard in that drawl. Yet, I would receive a rough slap on my plump behind if I didn't move fast enough.

I miss her.

1 Corinthians 13:13 – And now these three remain: faith, hope, and love. But the greatest of these is love.

Time Changes Things

What memories do you have from your past that bring you hope or joy? Who were the people that were your role models? How are you wiser today than when you were younger?

_____

_____

_____

_____

_____

_____

_____

_____

_____

_____

_____

_____

_____

_____

_____

_____

Praise Forward

Obedience Detected

The enemy comes
To Destroy
To Kill
and
To Steal.

God has come
To Love Me
To Guide Me
and
Be My Shield.

No time
For Laziness
Business
Negativity
or
Continued Delays.

I must
Think
Be Still
Listen
and
Pray.

Get Busy.
Time To Do!
Stop
Waiting
Complaining
and
Being Scared.

MOVE!

1 Corinthians 13:13 – And now these three remain: faith, hope, and love. But the greatest of these is love.

Obedience Detected

Do you allow disappointments to become a roadblock instead of a stepping stone? What is keeping you from accomplishing the goals that you set?

_____
_____
_____
_____
_____
_____
_____
_____
_____
_____
_____
_____
_____
_____
_____
_____

Self-Love

Brave
Beautiful
Bold
Brilliant

I command attention
When I stroll into a room.
I stand with confidence
And hold hands with grace.

Fabulous
Feisty
Forgiven
Faithful

I know I walk
with Victory.

It is etched
Into my DNA.
I am Favored
And Blessed.

Powerful
Purposeful
Pushy
And
Poised

Loving myself
Even when no
One else will.
Speaking words
Of positivity
To renew my soul.

1 Corinthians 13:13 – And now these three remain: faith, hope, and love. But the greatest of these is love.

Self-Love

Think about the words you say to yourself. Are they positive or negative? What kind of atmosphere do you want to create with the words you say?

_____

_____

_____

_____

_____

_____

_____

_____

_____

_____

_____

_____

_____

_____

_____

_____

Speak

Boldness
Power
Truth
Peace
Love

You're
Phenomenal
You're
Amazing
You're
Spectacular

Passionate
Fearless
Fierce
Brilliant

Stop
Allowing
Others
To Tell
Your
Story

1 Corinthians 13:13 – And now these three remain: faith, hope, and love. But the greatest of these is love.

Speak

What is YOUR story? What do you have to say to yourself, to the world, or to God? How do you want to say it?

_____
_____
_____
_____
_____
_____
_____
_____
_____
_____
_____
_____
_____
_____
_____
_____
_____

Jesus Will Fix It

Give him your burdens
Give him your brokenness
Trust him with your trials

Trust him with your tears
Tell him about your frustrations
Tell him about your failures

He will listen
He will hold you
He will order your steps
He will answer

He never promised
Everything would be easy
He never said
Trials wouldn't come

God will always
Be by your side
His love and mercy
He will never hide

Though trouble walks
In your pathway
Trust Jesus to
Always make a way

Out of darkness
Out of the pit
Out of the tears
Out of the pain

Jesus will fix it
Just call his name

1 Corinthians 13:13 – And now these three remain: faith, hope, and love. But the greatest of these is love.

Jesus Will Fix It

What worries do you need to give to God? Write down everything you are going through and talk to God about all of it.

_____
_____
_____
_____
_____
_____
_____
_____
_____
_____
_____
_____
_____
_____
_____
_____
_____

Praise Forward

Lean on Me

Worshipping In The Darkness
Listening To His Call
Depending On the Spirit
Praying Through The Storms

God's Grace
God's Favor
God's Mercy
God's Love

Praising Before The Breakthrough
Following His Instructions
Focusing On The Positive
Trusting In His Direction

God's Purpose
God's Power
God's Peace
God's Promises

Looking Beyond Yourself
Believing Without Seeing
Acting Out of Obedience
Expecting A Miracle

1 Corinthians 13:13 – *And now these three remain: faith, hope, and love. But the greatest of these is love.*

Lean on Me

Create a list of worship songs that you can go back to when you need them. Read the following scriptures and write down the promises that God shares with you. Jeremiah 29:11, Isaiah 40:31, Matthew 11:28-30, and Joshua 1:9

Section VI
Joy

"Daddy, I praise you for waking me up and giving me one more day! I praise you because you allowed the sun to shine and the birds to sing. I praise you because in spite of all that is going on in the world, you continue to bless me. You continue to help me be a blessing to others. I praise you for helping me through my valleys. You comforted me when I felt like giving up. I praise you for healing my body when I was sick. I praise you for reminding me to stop masking my pain and deal with issues holding me hostage. I praise you for reminding me that you are my strength, when I am weak. I have a new dance because of your goodness! I praise you because on the other side of my trials are my testimonies. Thank you Lord for keeping me. In Jesus name, Amen."

Psalm 118:24 - The Lord has done it this very day; let us rejoice today and be glad.

Sing

Sing about the raindrops coming down. Sing about your failures and your triumphs. Sing because you would never understand how good things really are until you know how bad things could get. Sing because it takes the rain to help you grow, dig deeper roots, bend, and not break in the wind. Sing because the stuff that made you cry yesterday only makes you stronger today. Sing, dance, and pray!

Psalm 118:24 – The Lord has done it this very day; let us rejoice today and be glad.

Sing

What song do you have in your heart? What small or big thing can you rejoice about in your life?

_____
_____
_____
_____
_____
_____
_____
_____
_____
_____
_____
_____
_____
_____
_____
_____
_____
_____

Still Here

The sun is shining and we are still here. Let us be thankful that we serve a God that still loves us through all our mistakes, issues, and complaining. Thankful for his protection last night while we were sleeping. Thankful for time to relax, refocus, and rejuvenate.

Psalm 118:24 – The Lord has done it this very day; let us rejoice today and be glad.

Still Here

This day has a purpose. What's yours? What will you accomplish? Pray, plan, and activate your purpose.

___
___
___
___
___
___
___
___
___
___
___
___
___
___
___
___
___

Soar

Stop Doing
And
Saying
Things that limit
Your capacity
To Grow
To Learn
And
To Produce
In Our Community
In Our World.
Stop Squashing
Your Potential
With Mediocrity
And Complacency.
Use Your
Brain Power.
Create Beauty.
Engage in Social Action.
Propel Political Change.
God can use
Anyone
Anywhere
Anytime
For His Glory.

Psalm 118:24 – The Lord has done it this very day; let us rejoice today and be glad.

Soar

It's time for you to fly! Take the next step to engage in your school, neighborhood, or community. What words and actions will you choose today, as you get ready to soar?

_____
_____
_____
_____
_____
_____
_____
_____
_____
_____
_____
_____
_____
_____
_____
_____
_____
_____

Choices

Life ain't going the way I figured, but I choose to smile. Some dreams were shattered and broken, but I choose to keep believing. Some events have occurred that placed me in a valley of depression, doubt, and disillusionment, but I choose to push and pray. Life does not always give you what you want, but God always gives you a choice. I choose victory, favor, and joy. I know I have them because God says so.

Psalm 118:24 – The Lord has done it this very day; let us rejoice today and be glad.

Choices

If life has been extremely difficult in the last few days, months, or years, choose to focus on the good and let God take care of the rest. Make a list things that you can choose to focus on that are positive.

_____

_____

_____

_____

_____

_____

_____

_____

_____

_____

_____

_____

_____

_____

_____

_____

Hallelujah Anyhow

Woke up

Able to move
Able to talk
Able to see
Able to hear

Food in my fridge
Roof over my head
Clothes on my back
People who love me

There's been pain
There's been death
There's been depression
There's been celebration

Sun in the morning
Rain during the day
Flowers are blooming
Moon shines at night

Breathing
I'm still alive
World is a mess
God still provides

Psalm 118:24 – The Lord has done it this very day; let us rejoice today and be glad.

Hallelujah Anyhow

Who and what do you have left after you thought it was all gone? How will you celebrate the things and people that remain?

_____
_____
_____
_____
_____
_____
_____
_____
_____
_____
_____
_____
_____
_____
_____
_____
_____

With Us

God is with us! He is with us in the valleys and on the mountains. He is with us today, yesterday, and tomorrow. Even when we walk away, God is still there. He is able to lighten your load of worry, pain, and frustration, if you give them to him. Allow him to guide you through your storms. Be grateful that they will not last forever. Hold on! You will find joy, again.

Psalm 118:24 – The Lord has done it this very day; let us rejoice today and be glad.

With Us

What have you been trying that never helps? What do you need to release to God? Write a letter to God asking for help. Expect him to answer.

_____
_____
_____
_____
_____
_____
_____
_____
_____
_____
_____
_____
_____
_____
_____
_____
_____

No Fear

God is
Your Strength
God Is
Your Power
God is
Your Hope

Be Bold
Be Courageous
Be Victorious

Keep Praying
Keep Listening
Keep Fighting

Talk Like It!
Walk Like It!
Act Like It!

Psalm 118:24 – The Lord has done it this very day; let us rejoice today and be glad.

No Fear

Tell fear to take a hike! You're not going to entertain him anymore. When he is no longer a roommate in your mind, what will you do differently?

_____
_____
_____
_____
_____
_____
_____
_____
_____
_____
_____
_____
_____
_____
_____
_____
_____
_____
_____

Inventory

I dare you to give thanks, when your heart is broken, or life seems upside down. Be excited about what is right in front of you. Reflect on a ime when God helped you through hard times, an addiction, or grief. Look at the pages of your life and see how he has guided during your highs and lows. Never forget the lessons you learned and your latest testimony.

Psalm 118:24 – The Lord has done it this very day; let us rejoice today and be glad.

Inventory

Learn to praise God during the trials and triumphs. What ways can you give glory to God even in the midst of what you are facing, right now? Why is it important to seek God in good and bad seasons of your life?

_____
_____
_____
_____
_____
_____
_____
_____
_____
_____
_____
_____
_____
_____
_____
_____

Praise Forward

Victory

Stay focused! You need to know that our God always has one more move. Even if the devil tries to block your shot, steal your joy, or run over your dreams, he can't stop you. You are a child of the King! It's championship time, so don't allow the enemy to defeat you. God has it all under control. Just because you can't see the master playbook that he's been working with doesn't mean he has forgotten you. Keep the faith and use your instruction booklet. You only have to run your plays, so let him worry about the rest. He will guide you, in due season, towards victory.

Psalm 118:24 – The Lord has done it this very day; let us rejoice today and be glad.

Victory

Sometimes we forget and try to run other people's plays on the court. We forget the position that God told us to play. How will you refocus on what God has called you to do?

_____
_____
_____
_____
_____
_____
_____
_____
_____
_____
_____
_____
_____
_____
_____
_____
_____
_____
_____

Shine

Search
For those
Who need
A smile.

Help
A Friend,
Neighbor,
Or Stranger.

Initiate
Time with
The Lost
Lonely
And Alone.

Share
The 'Gift of You'
Daily.

Never
Let anyone
Steal
Your light!

Psalm 118:24 – The Lord has done it this very day; let us rejoice today and be glad.

Shine

What is stopping you from SHINING? What are you willing to do to get your SHINE back?

_____
_____
_____
_____
_____
_____
_____
_____
_____
_____
_____
_____
_____
_____
_____
_____

Also Available by Synthia Shelby
PRAISE: In My Pocket!

Schedule Synthia for a speaking engagement:
Email: shelbyempowerment@gmail.com

Connect with Synthia online:
Website: www.synthiashelby.com

www.ingramcontent.com/pod-product-compliance
Lightning Source LLC
Chambersburg PA
CBHW070648160426
43194CB00009B/1628